SUMMARY

EAT

TO BEAT

DISEASE

The New Science of How Your Body Can Heal Itself.

By

William W Li

GREAT LIBERTY PUBLISHING

Disclaimer:

The information provided in this book is designed to provide helpful information on the subjects discussed.

WARNING: This book has passed copyscape and is free from plagiarism. False Copyright Claims will result in legal action taken.

Table of Contents

EXECUTIVE SUMMARY

We are really at a turning point in the fight against various diseases. Each of us has a tremendous opportunity to take charge of our lives using food to transform our health. You can make decisions about what to eat and drink based on the scientific evidence from food testing with the same systems and methods used to discover and develop drugs. The data generated when we study foods such as drugs clearly show that foods can affect our health in a specific and beneficial way. Blood vessels are beneficial to health because they bring oxygen and nutrients to every cell in our body.

Judah Folkman was a brilliant surgeon-scientist at Harvard. He was convinced that attacking the abnormal blood vessels that feed the cancer could be a totally new way of treating the disease. The angiogenesis that went wrong is not only a cancer problem, but also a common denominator for over seventy different diseases, including the leading causes of death in the world: stroke, Alzheimer's disease, heart disease, diabetes, Obesity and more.

We had a lot of success. A new field of medicine called angiogenesis-based therapy has been developed, as a result of coordinating collective efforts. Some of the innovative treatments prevent blood vessels from growing in diseased tissue, such as cancer or the blindness of diseases such as age-related neovascular macular degeneration and diabetic retinopathy. Other treatments that have changed medical practice are activating new blood vessels to heal vital tissues, such as in venous leg ulcers and diabetic ulcers. Currently, more than 32 drugs, medical devices and tissue products approved by the FDA are based on angiogenesis.

But, despite all the successes, the alarming fact is that the rate of new diseases is skyrocketing. Noncommunicable diseases, such as cancer, heart disease, stroke, diabetes, obesity and neurodegenerative diseases, are the major health threats to people around the world. Even with significant progress in FDA treatment and approval, treating the disease alone is not a sustainable solution for noncommunicable diseases, in part because of the stratospheric cost of new drugs. Pharmacological treatments alone cannot keep us healthy. Food can.

All doctors know that malnutrition is linked to a preventable disease and that food is becoming an increasingly important issue in the medical community. Few doctors know how to discuss a healthy diet with their patients. This is not the fault of individual doctors, but rather a side effect of the little nutritional education they receive. What all of this means to you is that your doctor, although endowed with deep skills and valuable knowledge about medicine, does not tell you what to eat so that your health can conquer the disease.

To understand the health benefits of foods, we must first understand the definition of health. For most people, health is the absence of disease. But it's much more than that. In fact, the definition of health requires a major update. What is clear is that our health is an active state, protected by a series of extraordinary defense systems in the body that are activated in all cylinders, from birth to the last day of life, allowing our cells and organs to function without problems.

These health defense systems are wired into our bodies to protect us. Some are so powerful that they can even reverse diseases such as cancer. And even though they function as separate defense systems, they also support and interact. These defense systems are the common denominators of health. By recalibrating our approach to disease prevention and focusing on these common denominators, we can take a unified approach to intercept diseases before they occur. It can be as powerful as finding common denominators for treating diseases, as we did two decades ago. Each of the systems is influenced by the diet. When you know what to eat to support each health promotion action, you know how to use your diet to stay healthy and conquer the disease. Think of your sanitary defense systems as the hidden defenses of the body's strength. These defenses caring for the body from the inside, it is now possible to systematically examine how to consolidate your health. The five defense systems are angiogenesis, regeneration, microbiome, DNA protection and immunity.

Part 1: HARD WIRED FOR HEALTH
Our Body's Natural Defense

Chapter 1

Angiogenesis

Key takeaway

1. Health is not simply the absence of disease. Health is an active state.

2. Your body has five health defense systems to maintain our health and to withstand the dangers we all face daily in our daily lives. They heal us when diseases cause us harm.

3. Your diet can be used to prevent illness, as well as to help with treatment.

Each of us, even if you have cancer that develops in our body. Up to ten thousand errors occur each day in the DNA of cells that divide in your body, making cancer formation not only common, but inevitable.

Your body has an extraordinary defense system that reduces microscopic cancers by depriving them of the blood supply and nutrients they need to develop. You can optimize this defense system with the food you consume.

Over a hundred foods can enhance your body's ability to defeat cancer and keep these tumors small and harmless, including tomatoes, soy, black raspberries, pomegranates and even some amazing ones, such as the liquorice, beer and cheese. You will find your defense weapons to ward off these tumors at the supermarket, at the farmers' market and in your garden.

Angiogenesis at work.

In every human body, there are 60,000 miles of blood vessels whose role is to provide oxygen and nutrients to keep cells alive. It is the vessels of life that nourish our healthy organs and protect us from disease.

The importance of angiogenesis for maintaining life is so fundamental that it starts in the reproductive system even before conception. When a sperm meets an egg, the uterus has already been prepared with the endometrium, a lining of new blood vessels ready to receive and feed the fertilized egg.

The defense against angiogenesis is a method to protect all animals with a circulatory system, including man. Any time you have had a deep cut as a result of surgery or trauma, you will no doubt have noticed that the injured area begins to undergo changes in seconds, initiating a process that continues until 'to healing the wound. Hypoxia causes injured cells to begin transmitting protein signals, called growth factors, whose role is to stimulate angiogenesis.

The angiogenesis system continuously detects where and when more vessels are needed to keep the organs healthy and functioning. As a prime contractor, the blood vessels feel the need for their muscles after a workout: it takes more blood flow to develop the muscles. On the other hand, the system is also constantly attentive to situations in which the blood vessels must be cut upside down. A healthy angiogenesis system, designed to achieve this goal, is neither small nor very small, but the balance and the right combination of blood vessels, twenty-four hours a day. The control of your body's angiogenesis needs to be perfect to optimize your health.

Helping the body prevent undesirable angiogenesis can have a powerful effect of suppressing cancer. The goal is to increase the defenses of angiogenesis, by helping your body's natural countermeasures keep the blood vessels in the normal equilibrium zone, which means that the cancer cells do not have the benefit of 'to be nourished, so they cannot grow.

Excessive angiogenesis causes disease in many other conditions than cancer, such as vision loss. Angiogenesis in the eye is so tightly controlled that the endothelial cells lining the blood vessels of the retina normally divide only twice in a person's life. Fortunately, these conditions can now be treated with FDA-approved biologics that ophthalmologists inject into the eye to stop destructive angiogenesis, leaks, and vision protection.

Even obesity has a strong link between angiogenesis. Although obesity is a multifactorial disease, overeating and eating the wrong foods generate high levels of growth factors that stimulate angiogenesis that circulates in the blood.

People with diabetes can develop a compromised nervous blood supply, especially if your blood sugar is not well managed. Diabetes also decreases angiogenesis, which damages the nerves. When your defenses of angiogenesis are paralyzed, many other diseases can interfere with your life. Chronic wounds are another example. While normal wounds heal in less than a week, chronic wounds are slow to heal or do not heal at all. These open wounds become infected, gangrenous and often result in the need to amputate an affected limb. If you have a chronic wound, one of the main goals of your doctor should be to start angiogenesis to improve blood flow and accelerate healing. This can be done with a variety of medical devices and other techniques, like diet.

Your heart and brain also depend on the defense system of angiogenesis to react whenever your own circulation is threatened. To quickly restore blood flow to these organs is literally a matter of life and death.

Food and angiogenesis

Dieting can be used for disease prevention as well as to help with treatment. Research around the world shows that certain foods and beverages, including those we recognize and enjoy, can strengthen the defenses of angiogenesis on both sides of the equation. Even the way you prepare and combine the ingredients in foods can influence angiogenesis. This gives a completely new perspective on how to think what foods you eat and how to eat them.

In Asia, people who consume a lot of soy, vegetables and tea have a much lower risk of developing breast cancer or other types of cancer. In Japan, there are more than sixty-nine thousand people over one hundred years old. China also has a growing population of centenarians.

The dynamic centenarians of Ikaria, Greece and central Sardinia eat the Mediterranean diet, which is full of ingredients that stimulate the defense of angiogenesis and are not strictly vegan.

Chapter 2

Regeneration

Key takeaway

1. Stem cells develop and maintain organs and are so vital to your health that if they suddenly stop functioning, you will be dead within a week.

2. Whether you are an athlete who is developing his muscles or a pregnant mother who is developing a fetus, or a person struggling with the ravages of aging, the right foods can help increase the amount and performance of your stem cells and their ability to regenerate your body.

3. We can avoid some risks for our stem cells by reducing our exposure to air pollution, tobacco and alcohol. Better control of blood sugar. But some other risks are more difficult to avoid. Aging, for example, is constantly reducing our ability to regenerate.

Stem cells grow and maintain organs and are so vital to your health that if they stop working suddenly, you will die within a week. From conception, stem cells have played a key role in the generation and maintenance of your body and your health. We are literally made of stem cells. Stem cells of the fetus not only build the body, but also ensure the health of even the mother.

The critical roles played by stem cells in adult life: your small intestine is regenerated every 2 to 4 days, your lungs and your stomach, every 8 days, your skin, every 2 weeks, your red blood cells, every 4 months, your fat cells, every 8 years, your skeleton, every 10 years.

The Healing Power of Stem Cells

Bone marrow transplant is a rescue procedure practiced worldwide to rescue cancer patients treated with the most severe chemotherapy and the highest doses of radiation. Although chemotherapy and radiation destroy cancer cells, they also destroy healthy bone marrow stem cells. Without stem cells, the immune system of the cancer patient is blocked and it can die from an overwhelming infection. However, by transplanting stem cells taken from the bone marrow of a donor to a cancer patient, doctors can save patients from this certain death.

Of the 37.2 billion cells in your body, stem cells are a small but powerful subset, only 0.002%, that can regenerate your health. Stem cells replace, repair and regenerate dead and worn cells on demand. And, like the angiogenesis system, the latest research shows that stem cells are strongly influenced by diet.

If you're an athlete who is developing your muscles or a pregnant mother who builds a fetus, or someone who fights the ravages of aging, the right foods can help increase the amount and performance of your stem cells and your abilities, to regenerate your body.

Stem Cells and Injury

What stem cells do exactly once they are embedded in the injured tissue remains a mystery. We know that they differentiate and regenerate the local tissue. But stem cells do not stay long. They last only a few days at most.

The Regeneration Defense System is programmed to be ready at any time to respond to an injury or trauma. Adult stem cells are not specialized, they remain on hold until they are needed and implemented. They can be renewed and replicated by cell division while maintaining their pluripotency. When they are in mission mode, they perceive their environment and use the signals around them to give instructions, become the exact type of cell that needs to be regenerated. If they are in a lung, they become lungs. If they are in the liver, they become liver.

Bone marrow is a storage unit for at least three types of stem cells: hematopoietic stem cells (HSCs), mesenchymal stromal cells (MSCs) and endothelial progenitor cells (EPCs).

When stem cells are called to act by a part of the body that needs to be regenerated, a series of events is carried out to bring the stem cell from its niches to its circulatory system. Once they have joined the landing zone, the stem cells assess the environment of the organ in which they landed and carry out their mission according to the instructions given by their environment.

Causes of stem cell damage

One of the most harmful is tobacco smoke. The smoking habit reduces the number of stem cells stored in the bone marrow by 80%, leaving fewer cells available for regeneration and repair over time, increasing the risk of cardiovascular and pulmonary diseases. Even if you do not smoke yourself, you are not sure of being close to those who do it.

Excess alcohol kills stem cells. Alcohol affects stem cells in many ways. Fetal Alcohol Syndrome is a disastrous consequence when pregnant women consume a lot of alcohol. The developing fetus suffers from permanent brain damage and growth abnormalities. Since alcohol is toxic to fetal stem cells, fetal alcohol syndrome could be devastated in part by damaged stem cells. Chronic diseases can also have a detrimental effect on stem cells. Diabetes kills stem cells. People with diabetes have fewer stem cells and those that exist cannot do their job properly.

Diabetes is one of the leading causes of strokes, heart attacks, blindness, kidney failure, chronic wounds and disability caused by lower limb amputations. These are all medical complications related in one way or another to dysfunctional stem cells. Any method to protect or improve stem cell performance in diabetes, hyperlipidemia and aging could save lives.

We can avoid certain risks to our stem cells by reducing our exposure to air pollution, smoking and alcohol, as well as better control of blood sugar levels. But some other risks are more difficult to avoid. Aging, for example, is constantly reducing our ability to regenerate.

Benefits of Boosting Stem Cells

If we take steps to stimulate our stem cells, the effects on our health can be positive. In its cardiovascular system, stem cells have unique protective functions. Endothelial progenitor cells not only contribute to the formation of new blood vessels during organ regeneration, but also play an important role in repairing damage in existing blood vessels.

If damage to the lining is not repaired, more and more plaque will accumulate, eventually accumulating to reduce the diameter of the blood vessel and close the blood flow. Damage to the stem cells therefore reduces their regenerative defenses against atherosclerosis. Maintaining healthy stem cells reduces the risk of atherosclerotic accumulation and protects against the development of cardiovascular disease.

The loss of brain stem cells is involved in the development of dementia. These stem cells, called progenitor oligodendrocytes, regenerate and replace neurons in your brain and are essential for maintaining acute mental function as you get older.

Stem cells in medicine

The benefits of stem cells in health is undeniable and clinical trials are underway around the world to develop stem cell therapies. Although there are many ways to create regenerative therapy, a common method is to inject stem cells into the body to improve organ regeneration for heart, eye, kidney, pancreas and liver diseases. Common sources for stem cells used in these treatments are blood, bone marrow, fat and even skin.

Another approach to attract a patient's stem cells to recovery is to emit ultrasound on the skin. Regenerative medicine is already changing the way medicine is practiced and will find new ways of overcoming diseases that are now considered irritating and unbeatable.

Food and stem cells

Now you can start the regenerative defense of your body in your kitchen. Foods and beverages can activate a person's own stem cells, increasing the body's ability to regenerate and heal itself from within.

This approach to regeneration is completely new and requires no doctor, hospital or injection. Food regeneration takes advantage of its own reservoir of stem cells to restore health. Some foods enhance stem cell activity and promote regeneration, while other foods damage stem cells, rendering them powerless.

Chapter 3

Microbiome

Key takeaway

1. Our microbiota can mean the difference between life and death, between developing or resisting serious illness.

2. Foods have a surprising ability to influence these powers of the microbiome. After all, our bacteria eat what we eat.

3. As for human communities, the diversity of our bacterial ecosystem provides strength and more effective collaborations to protect health.

4. Our microbiome influences our health in many ways, including the substances they produce by processing the food that passes through our gut.

5. Your microbiome extends throughout the body, especially in skin and body cavities.

The term holobiont describes an organism functioning as a set of mutually beneficial

24

multiple species. You are a holobiont because your body is not a singular entity, but an extremely complex ecosystem comprising 39 billion bacteria, mostly good bacteria, that abound in and on the surface of your body. Although the medical community once thought that microorganisms collectively called the microbiome a vector of unpleasant diseases that needed to be cleaned, sterilized and killed with antibiotics, we now know that most of the bacteria in our body work in sophisticated ways to influence our behavior and defend our health. Some bacteria release metabolites that can protect against diabetes, influence angiogenesis, stem cells and immunity and even affect our hormones, sexual condition and social behavior. They can feed our human cells or irritate and inflame them.

The relationship between man and bacteria: good and bad

Humans have evolved with bacteria on this planet. At the dawn of the Homosapiens, three hundred thousand years ago, our hunter-gatherer ancestors ate what they could look for: nuts, cereals, legumes and ancient fruits, which contain all the high amounts of fiber in which the microbes develop. The food was collected by hand in the soil and the vegetation laden with bacteria. Every bite swallowed by our distant ancestors was therefore laden with microbes from the environment and entering their innards. Humans did not even know that even bacteria existed, let alone that they were aware of the role healthy bacteria play in our bodies. But over the past centuries, science has transformed our understanding of how bacteria contribute to both disease and health.

However, there was an unexpected consequence. The more people learned to control and eliminate bacteria that could cause an infection, the more widespread the idea that all bacteria were harmful. Thus, began the era of germaphobia that continues today.

To unravel the mysteries of the human microbiome, in 2008 the National Institutes of Health launched the Human Microbiome project, inspired by the Human Genome Project.

 The project published a historical article in the prestigious scientific journal Nature in 2012, which documents the bacteria of the microbiome of 242 people.

The diversity of microbiomes is an important seal of health. As with human communities, the diversity of our bacterial ecosystem provides strength and more effective collaborations to protect health. The more numerous and varied bacteria we have, the healthier we become. Our microbiome influences our health in many ways, including the substances they produce when they process food that passes through our intestines. The best-known substances are actually bacterial metabolites called short-chain fatty acids (SCFAs). Other microbial metabolites can also promote health. Lactobacillus plantarum bacteria, for example, produce metabolites that stimulate an anti-inflammatory response by intestinal stem cells.

Its microbiome spreads throughout the body, especially in skin and body cavities. Bacteria that promote health are found in the gums, teeth, tongue and tonsils, as well as in the lungs, nose, ears, vagina and, in particular, the intestines.

But as we learn how our microbiome defends our health, we are thinking about how changing our gut bacteria could contribute to the mysterious rates of food allergies, obesity, diabetes, cardiovascular disease, cancer, Alzheimer's disease and even depression. The riddle is far from over, but it should make us more cautious about the risky use of antibiotics and even antiseptics. And that tells us that we should think more about how to keep our gut bacteria healthy for our overall health. What you eat is number one approach in achieving your goal.

The functioning of the gut microbiome is strongly influenced by our diet. During his lifetime, sixty tons of food will pass through your digestive tract. What you eat also nourishes your bacteria. Prebiotic foods can improve bacterial function. We can also introduce new bacteria into our ecosystem by eating foods that naturally contain healthy microbes. This can easily be achieved by eating common fermented foods. However, these are probiotic foods. Other foods modify the intestinal environment, making the growth of certain bacteria more favorable.

We are constantly introducing new bacteria into our bodies, even exchanging bacteria with friends and family members, who are then part of our microbiome. A kiss can introduce up to 80 million bacteria per kiss. But the most common entry point is to eat. Foods that affect the microbiome are probiotic or prebiotic. Another way our food can affect the microbiome is to alter the gut environment so that it is conducive to the growth of healthy bacteria. Think about the species of bacteria in the gut as competing sports teams. Each of them trains and prepares to compete with each other to gain dominance. Giving species the foods, they prefer can boost their growth relative to other team, giving them a competitive advantage.

Some foods can affect the mucosal lining and help these bacteria improve their environment. Akkermansia is an important beneficial bacterium in our microbiome. It lives and thrives perfectly in the mucous membrane of the intestinal mucus and can be increased by eating foods such as cranberries or pomegranates.

Our way of eating can actually force the extinction of some gut bacteria, which can affect the health of future generations. Even in the short term, unhealthy diets wreak havoc on your microbiome and leave a scar that takes time to recover even after returning to a healthier diet. These scars can create serious imbalances for your health. Because the microbiome is linked to other health defense systems, an unhealthy diet can, by extension, damage its defense against angiogenesis, disrupt the functioning of stem cells, hinder the protection of your body's DNA and compromise your immune system.

Although modern civilization has devoted most of the twentieth century to the fight against diseases caused by microbes, in the twenty-first century, we can fight this disease by using a bacterium, for example a bacterium called Lactobacillus reuteri, a species that is part of the human microbiome and can make injury to heal faster, reduction of abdominal fat, obesity in mice stimulates the growth of thick, shiny and healthy hair; improve the tone of the skin; strengthens the immune system; and prevent the growth of tumors in the colon and in the chest.

The biotechnology industry is eager to harness the power of the microbiome. A procedure called fecal microbial transplantation (FMT) has been developed to treat dysbiosis by replacing unhealthy intestinal bacteria with useful intestinal bacteria from the feces of a healthy donor. The procedure has been used to treat patients with Clostridium difficile colitis, a complication often related to the use of antibiotics, as explained above. Some biotech companies are developing special formulas for probiotics, dietary fiber and bioactive smoothie plants to promote the growth of healthy bacteria in the gut as a way to treat diabetes, obesity and other conditions.

Diet can be the most powerful tool to influence our microbiome. Natural foods offer a more diverse source, such as yogurt, fermented foods and some beverages loaded with bacteria. But even when you do not directly consume probiotic bacteria, what we eat has the deepest effect of every day on our defense system against the microbiome. Our diet can reduce or increase different populations of gut microbiota hour by hour. The foods you eat affect the ability of your gut to heal, sometimes surprisingly.

Chapter 4
DNA protection

Key takeaway

1. Protecting our DNA is essential if we want to be healthy.

2. Our DNA is programmed to defend and protect itself, and therefore our health, from the toxic chemicals in the air we breathe, in the foods we eat and, otherwise, we absorb through our skin the products from home and other environmental sources.

3. When our DNA is damaged for any reason, errors can occur in the way our genetic instructions are followed in the body. When mutations are inherited from our genes, disastrous diseases can occur.

4. The amount of damage to DNA that occurs every day is incredible, but our DNA has been programmed to repair most of the damage before it becomes a problem.

5. A good night's sleep results in epigenetic changes in DNA, so does pulling an all-nighter, but one is good and the other bad.

We know that DNA is your personal genetic model. It is twisted in the form of a spiral staircase (called a double helix) and miniaturized to fit into a cell. The staircase is a collection of the genes you inherited from your parents. It's the source code on which all aspects of your health depend to keep it alive and allow it to function normally.

Your DNA contains more than ten thousand harmful events that occur naturally each day. Some of these errors are spontaneous interruptions that happen by chance when billions of cells work and replicate without stopping, day after day. Other mistakes are a side effect of something destructive happening inside the body, such as inflammation or infection. And even more as a result of the presence of toxic chemicals in the air we breathe, in the foods we eat and, otherwise, we absorb household products and other environmental sources through the skin. our DNA is connected to defend and protect itself, and therefore your health, against the consequences of this damage.

Day after day, much of what you hear about DNA refers to ancestry, but significant advances in genetic detection can detect your personal risk of hereditary cancers and other diseases. When mutations are inherited from our genes, disastrous diseases can occur. As we age, our DNA wears out. Throughout our lives, the choices we make: where we live, what we eat, our way of life, either helps or damages our DNA. Protecting our DNA is essential if we want to be healthy.

Our DNA uses different mechanisms to protect itself. Our cells have evolved with powerful repair processes that continuously monitor our DNA to detect structural abnormalities.

The telomeres are like aglets, the lids covering the ends of the laces of the shoes, sitting at both ends of the chromosomes. Protect your DNA from wear with age. Good nutrition, regular exercise, quality sleep, and other healthy activities can protect your telomeres.

The source code of the DNA is written in chemical substances whose name begins with one of the following four letters: A (adenine), T (thymine), C (cytosine) or G (guanine). The steps of the spiral staircase consist of different combinations of pairs of these letters (A-T and

C-G). A sequence of these pairs that encodes instructions for a complete protein is known as a gene, which would be similar to a group of steps on the spiral staircase. Surprisingly, every cell in your body knows how to read this source code. The cells use the code when downloading into a cellular device that acts as a miniature 3D printer and makes proteins out of the code. The production of these proteins occurs behind the scenes, in silence, every second of your life, from the moment you were conceived at the time of your death.

Many external factors are threats because they can interrupt and damage our source code. Although the industry creates many hazards, not all threats are caused by humans. One of the most damaging factors for DNA is ultraviolet radiation. The sun is not the only threat. Harmful radiation also emanates from the ground. It is in the form of radon, an odorless natural gas that enters homes through basements. Different parts of the Earth emit different levels of radon, but it is an invisible invader that damages the DNA. In fact, radon is the leading cause of lung cancer in nonsmokers. Solvents are released from carpets, new cars and chemicals found in common household products, such as nail polish remover, shampoo and paint damage your DNA. These exposures alter the genes in sperm through epigenetic mechanisms, and the changes can be passed on to offspring.

Your cells contain repair enzymes that can detect and repair this type of damage. Enzymes come into play when they notice deviations from the ordered structure of the DNA double helix. Scientific and clinical research has shown that the consumption of certain foods can reduce DNA damage by increasing the speed and efficiency of the repair process after damage or prevent damage in the first place.

When the DNA repair system starts, the cell knows that it must limit the ripple effect of any damage that has occurred. As a result, it slows down the replication cycle that cells use to copy themselves, including their DNA. This ensures that the damaged DNA is less likely to be transmitted. If there is only a lot of damage to repair, a cell can trigger its own death through a process called apoptosis. It should be noted that biotechnology companies are exploring ways to leverage the DNA repair process used by bacteria to create new genetic treatments for a range of diseases in humans, plants and even insects.

Epigenetics answers the question of why and how every cell in our body has the same DNA, but we have so many different cells with various functionalities. The environment of the tissue around each cell is unique from one organ to another. Epigenetic expression is not fixed even in one organ. Your DNA responds to external influences both internal and external to the body, depending on the circumstances. Stress, mindfulness, sleep, the foods you eat (herbal foods), what you drink, exercise and pregnancy are just some of the internal circumstances that have an epigenetic influence.

Epigenetic influences on DNA are an important area of research, especially with respect to food, but before I tell what's going on with food, it's instructive to see how other activities related to lifestyle influence our genes through these changes. Most healthy activities create positive epigenetic changes and we now realize that this is how they give us their benefits through our genes.

Exercise, for example, causes epigenetic changes that release our genes to produce useful proteins for building muscle, increase the pumping capacity of the heart, develop new blood vessels to help muscle expansion and reduce blood lipids. Other epigenetic modifications in exercise can block harmful genes. They are seen after speed racing, swimming, interval training and high intensity walking. A good night's sleep results in epigenetic changes in DNA, as well as pulling an all-nighter, but one is good and the other bad.

Telomeres are the third part of the DNA defense team. These are the protective caps located at both ends of the chromosome DNA that help maintain the structure of the chromosomes and prevent them from sticking to each other. On the other hand, telomeres inevitably shorten during aging. Studies of people over sixty-five show that people with shorter telomeres die earlier than those with longer telomeres. Smoking, lack of sleep, high stress, and lack of exercise accelerate the wear of telomere capsules and reduce telomerase activity. Some foods, such as turmeric, soy, and coffee, can trigger protective genes while mitigating harmful effects. Some diets help protect and extend our telomeres, including the Mediterranean diet and the similar patterns that result.

What is fascinating is that people who live up to a hundred years old have telomere lengths that are unusual. Among the influences on telomeres, the diet is one of the most powerful. Remember the study of children who had longer telomeres because they were breastfed.

These are some of the conditions in which the defenses of DNA are violated: atherosclerosis, Alzheimer's disease, cancer (of all kinds), diabetes, cystic fibrosis, Li-Fraumeni syndrome, post-traumatic stress disorder, obesity, systemic erythema of lupus, autism, celiac disease, ataxia telangiectasia, depression, inflammatory bowel disease, Parkinson's disease, Lynch syndrome, rheumatoid arthritis, schizophrenia.

Chapter 5

Immunity

Key takeaway

1. Immunity is so powerful that it can protect you from cancer.

2. Immunity prevents us from infecting ourselves after a cut, fights viruses and prevents us from catching harmful microbes from a traveling companion on the bus.

3. The immune system is one of the pillars of the defense of health. It is designed to protect the body against the invasion of viruses, bacteria and parasites through an ingenious pattern recognition system.

4. Exercise, proper sleep and stress reduction and control help your immune system stay healthy.

A strong immune system helps prevent colds. But did you know that immunity is so powerful that it can protect you against cancer? And if you have cancer, your immune system is able to completely eliminate it from your body, even

SUMMARY: EAT TO BEAT DISEASE By William W Li

if it has spread. Genetics, smoking, the environment, poor nutrition and other factors are often attributed to cancer. But the truth is that, whatever its cause, cancer only becomes a disease when the malignant cells escape the destruction of our immune system. Our immune system is one of the best-known health defense systems. It prevents us from getting infected after a cut, fighting virus and catching harmful microbes that a passenger on the bus coughed out into the air.

At other times, the immune system weakens and can no longer do its job correctly, so the cancer cells are neglected and are able to grow. People who suffer from immunodeficiency, such as AIDS, or who have received an organ transplant and must take immune-suppressive steroids for life to prevent organ rejection, are at a very high risk of developing cancer because their system immune is compromised. New treatments for cancer immunotherapy help your immune system eliminate dangerous cancer cells. This approach is remarkable because it does not rely on toxic or specific drugs to kill cancer cells. Specific foods, as well as their components, can also strongly affect our immune defenses. It is clear that the immune system is one of the pillars of the defense of health. It is designed to protect the body from the invasion of viruses, bacteria and parasites through an ingenious pattern recognition system. Immune cells identify and destroy threats while recognizing healthy cells and leaving them alone. Under normal circumstances, in healthy people, the immune system is always in sleep mode, like the fire department, ready to act when an alarm sound. Your body automatically knows whether to increase or decrease your immune response. Neither inactive nor hyperactive, it operates from a point where all forces are balanced, but in a state of constant vigilance.

You can take many steps to protect your immune defenses throughout your life. Exercise, good sleep and stress reduction and control help to keep your immune system healthy. So can your diet choices.

When exposed to scabies (smallpox), the immune system began to mount a defense against the smallpox virus, giving the recipients an immunity to the disease. This crude technique was known as variolation (remember that the smallpox virus is called variola) and subsequently led to what is now called vaccination.

The power of your immune system lies in your military capabilities. Like the military, your immune system has different branches. Each branch has different types of soldiers with their own specialized training, their weapons and their skills to defend their homeland. Central control of immunity is found in four parts of the body: the bone marrow, the thymus, the spleen, and the lymph nodes and your gut.

The location of the fourth seat of immunity, the gut, is essential to understanding the connection between diet and immunity. The gut also contains the microbiome which, as we saw in Chapter 3, can affect the immune system. The importance of the bowel for immune defense has recently been recognized for its fundamental role in maintaining health. All cells come from bone marrow stem cells called hematopoietic stem cells. This is why medications such as chemotherapy, which damage bone marrow cells and circulating white blood cells, decrease your immunity. On the other hand, diet can affect the production of immune cells in bone marrow.

Our immune system is made up of two different immune systems, each designed in its own way to protect your body against foreign invaders, be they bacteria, viruses, parasites or cancer cells. One of them acts quickly, reacting immediately to an invading body attack. It is a blunt instrument, programmed to defend our body against any invader using the same weapons each time. It's the innate immune system. When you have an allergic reaction or inflammation, it's the innate system at work. The second immune system acts more slowly, but in a much more sophisticated way. This system takes about a week to assemble its defenses, but when it does, it is very well tuned to eliminate specific targets against invaders in the body. It is the adaptive (or acquired) immune system. It works in two main ways: it can defend itself by using specialized cells designed to kill, or it can create antibodies that swarm like hornets to surround and attack the enemy.

The innate immune system is the first to react to any invasion of your body. Act as a watchdog ready to take action as soon as a stranger enters your garden. This system is not selective and blocks and simply attacks everything in its path. Innate defense includes physical, chemical and cellular components. The cells in the innate system create inflammation, that is, a response of the body to tissue damage or foreign invasion. The inflammation causes specific immune cells at the site of the injury to keep the enemy locked and contained in a specific area, to kill the invaders, and then to get rid of their bodies. The innate immune response is short-lived and gives in a few days. When the time comes to reject the inflammatory response, a signal called interleukin 10, emitted by the immune system, disables the program and reduces the immune defenses to a normal state of health.

When you receive a vaccine to prevent a disease, such as the polio vaccine, your adaptive immune system is responsible for creating protection against the disease. The adaptive (or acquired) immune system is the most intelligent and sophisticated branch of your immune system. Unlike the innate system, which is a blunt instrument, the adaptive system is very selective in what it kills. And he has a permanent memory of the invaders he destroys. This memory helps the immune system to activate a rapid response team in case the enemy, be it a bacterium, a virus or a cancer, raises the head in the future.

Different foods influence different parts of the immune system. Some raise the defense, while others reject it. The diet tends to influence cell-mediated immunity, which involves T cells. Remember, there are three main types of T cells: helper T cells, cytotoxic T cells and suppressor T cells (also known as Tregs, because they dampen down the immune system).

Failure of your immune system at its job, will put your life in serious jeopardy. It is true that invasive bacteria and viruses sometimes escape our defenses. That's why you catch a cold or catch the flu. Massive attacks can come from outside the body or from the inside. Harmful microbes, for example, can enter our interior through the nose, eyes, mouth, ears, vagina or anus, through any orifice exposed to the outside world. And when there is a laceration, the opening in the skin is an open door for the microbes to enter the body mass. The best-known example of the collapse of life-threatening immunity is Acquired Immunodeficiency Syndrome (AIDS). AIDS is caused by infection with the human immunodeficiency virus (HIV), which infamously eliminates internal immunity. This leads to a high risk of catastrophic infections, as well as the growth of cancers. At the other end of the spectrum, an immune army that melts can turn against our health. Autoimmunity is the term used to describe a hyperactive immune system, where normal cells and organs are attacked and their function destroyed. Autoimmune diseases have no cause but are triggered by a number of factors. environment, Genetics, infections, drug reactions and changes in the microbiome have been associated with autoimmune diseases.

Other situations with exaggerated immune responses are observed in allergic reactions, such as asthma and food allergies. In cases of severe allergies, the immune system reacts excessively with an otherwise harmless allergen (pollen, food) introduced by the mucous membranes. The immune system that triggers the blow sees him as a foreign invader.

PART 2: EAT TO BEAT DISEASE
The Evidence for Food as Medicine

Key takeaway

1. Each of the five health defense systems in your body is intimately linked to your diet.

2. Research is revealing more and more evidence about how the food we eat can have a significant influence on these systems, which in turn activates their ability to maintain our good health or destroy them.

Chapter 6

Starve your disease, feed your health

Today, angioprevention refers to a health approach that includes the use of foods, medications and dietary supplements. Reducing red meat, Regular exercise, and sugar, and not smoking are solid approaches to avoiding disease, but they are only part of the solution. Using a diet (such as an Asian plant-based) to support and strengthen your body's angiogenesis defense system can reduce your risk of developing a full spectrum of dreaded diseases.

The goal of an angio-preventive regimen is to maintain the body's angiogenesis defense system in a state of healthy equilibrium. This is sometimes confusing for Western-trained physicians because balance is not usually part of their lexicon for treating the disease. Balance is a more familiar concept in traditional Ayurvedic medicine, where the focus is on balance for preventive health. Health is perceived in these systems as the presence of balanced systems in the body and mind. A state of balance is where you want to be at all times of your life.

Bioactive substances in foods and beverages are absorbed in small amounts, which can help influence the body's ability to maintain balanced angiogenesis. The anti-angiogenic factors present in the diet can only bring back the vessels in excess to the reference levels. This means that a food that causes hunger through cancer will not make the heart fail to get the necessary blood supply because it is about keeping the body on a healthy foundation. On the other side of the equation, foods that stimulate angiogenesis will not make blood vessels overgrow their natural limits in the circulatory system. Pro-angiogenic foods and beverages will not overuse the system and will not cause cancer. According to the principles of homeostasis, a diet of angiogenesis helps maintain the state of harmony and balance of the body.

Diseases Driven by Excessive Angiogenesis

There is a poorly recognized but important link between angiogenesis and coronary artery disease. The heart is a muscle that needs robust angiogenesis whenever its coronary arteries become clogged with cholesterol-laden plaque.

However, these plaques are not simply thick layers of mud that agglutinate in the walls of a blood vessel. These are true growths that, like tumors, depend on new blood vessels to dilate.

Cancer is one of the most feared diseases of all time. Each type of solid tumor, from the breast to the prostate through the lung and colon, must have angiogenesis to develop beyond a precise size. Without angiogenesis, cancer cells cannot spread either.

Up to 90-95% of cancers are related to environmental exposures and our lifestyle. About 30% of cancer deaths are diet related. Most researchers and cancer activists point out the harmful dietary factors to avoid to reduce the risk of cancer. Inculcating beverages, foods, and natural ingredients in your diet can reduce your risk of cancer.

Some foods in the world that can maintain balanced angiogenesis are: tomato, soy, antiangiogenic vegetables (such as bok choy, broccoli rabe, cauliflower and Romanesco) antiangiogenic fruits (such as peaches, nectarines, plums, apricots, berries , cherries), mango, cloudy apple cider and even lychee, seafood, beverages, chicken drumsticks, red wine, cheese, beer, olive oil, walnuts (pecan, walnuts, almonds, cashews , pistachios, pine nuts, macadamia) and beans, dark chocolate(cocoa), spices and herbs.

Diseases requiring more angiogenesis

Following a diet to stimulate the growth of blood vessels can help nourish your organs and prevent disease. Remember that food cannot cancel the body's own normal reference points for angiogenesis. This means that anti-angiogenic foods cannot reduce the number of blood vessels in the body needed to maintain the health of their organs. And it also means that foods that stimulate angiogenesis cannot outweigh your body's ability to keep excess blood vessels trimmed so they can not cause disease. Food can only help to improve the state of natural balance. By fueling the health defense of angiogenesis on both sides of the equation, you can eat to fight several diseases simultaneously.

Your cardiovascular system needs blood vessels to function at its optimal level. When there are not enough vessels to satisfy the circulatory demand of your brain, heart, legs or internal organs, the cells are starved of oxygen and become invalid. They will eventually die. Ischemic heart disease is caused by the narrowing of the coronary arteries that carry blood to the heart muscle.

Your brain may experience the same type of crisis. When the blood vessels of the brain become narrower, the brain cells become deprived of oxygen. It can also occur when the carotid arteries, the main trunks of the blood vessels that go from neck to brain, become clogged. The same narrowing that atherosclerosis of the heart and brain can also occur in the legs. This is called peripheral arterial disease and leads to inadequate blood flow to the lower limbs and feet. Chronic wounds begin with ulcers on the skin, usually on the legs and feet, which do not heal. People with diabetes are particularly prone to foot ulcers because the blood supply to the nerves of the foot is insufficient. The nerves suffer ischemic and can die.

Pressure ulcers (or bed sores) can occur in anyone who exerts excessive pressure and no relief, anywhere in the body. People who are bedridden and cannot move can develop these ulcers on their buttocks and near their tailbones.

Erectile dysfunction is a major problem for many men. There is a lot of underlying causes, but insufficient angiogenesis to help bring the blood to the pudendal nerve will permanently eliminate the function of the penis. Alopecia, or hair loss, may be due to insufficient growth of the blood vessels. Hair follicles need new blood vessels for their nutritional needs. When this is compromised, the hair is not replaced because it falls naturally from the scalp.

Foods that stimulate angiogenesis

Pro-angiogenic foods that can stimulate angiogenesis and improve blood flow.

Food like:

Grains and seeds

Foods containing ursolic acid, e.g. ginseng, rosemary, mint and fruit peels (dried fruit, such as cherries, sultana raisins, cranberries, and blueberries, including apple skin).

Foods rich in quercetin: foods like hot Green peppers, capers, red leaf lettuce, cranberries, onions, black plums and apples.

54

Chapter 7
(Re)generate Your Health

Key takeaway

1. Stem cells are always at work, but as you get older, they slow down and can use some help. Eating foods that mobilize your stem cells can increase your body's intrinsic ability to protect and maintain your organs.

2. Science tells us that we can fight the effects of aging by using foods that stimulate our stem cells to do what they did before in our youth.

3. Stem cells is known to repair and regenerate damaged blood vessels solely caused by aging and high cholesterol levels, thereby protecting cardiovascular health.

We all want to stay young and maintain our vitality for as long as possible so we can truly enjoy all that life has to offer. Even if you are not interested in living until you are a hundred years old, you still want to take a step back and be insightful. Science tells us that we can fight the effects of aging by using foods that stimulate our stem cells to do what they did in our youth. Simple aging causes a decrease in the number and strength of our stem cells and slows the body's ability to regenerate. Choosing the right foods can help you put your stem cells into action to help your muscles grow, maintain their vigor and reduce the ravages of aging. Stem cells keep you not only young, but can also regenerate tissue damage by aging. Although it may seem counter-intuitive that eating chocolate can reduce the risk of coronary heart disease, chocolate is a food that captures stem cells.

Stem cells from the bone marrow, heart, skin and other organs can be activated by what we eat and how we eat it. Eating regenerative foods makes you more fit from the inside and continues to rebuild your organs so they are in the best shape possible. Foods that mobilize stem cells help neutralize and prevent organ damage that inevitably develops with aging. Stem cells can also help reverse the ravages of cardiovascular disease, diabetes, smoking, hypercholesterolemia and obesity.

Foods that can help support the body's regenerative defense system (that is, they influence everything from repairing damaged organs to combating the effects of excessive fat consumption). Foods such as *Squid Ink, Fish*

Oil, Whole Wheat, Black Chokeberry, Green Beans, Rice Bran, Foods and Beverages High in Resveratrol (like grapes, red wine, blueberries, *Turmeric,* peanuts, cranberries, and even pistachios), Foods High in Zeaxanthin (like leafy green vegetables, like kale, mustard greens, watercress, spinach, collard greens, Swiss chard, and fiddleheads), Foods High in Chlorogenic Acid (like black tea, peaches, blueberries, fresh and dried plums, eggplants, and even bamboo shoots), *Black Raspberries, Chinese Celery and Mangoes.*

Stem cell stimulating drinks are beer, red wine, green tea and black tea. Stem cells: improve eating habits, such as the Mediterranean diet and caloric restriction and fasting.

Diets that harm beneficial stem cells such as: high fat diet, hyperglycemic foods and high salt diet.

Foods that kill cancer stem cells

Finding ways to kill cancer stem cells has been one of the secrets of cancer research. This is a goal sought by biotech companies specializing in the treatment of cancer, but scientists have already discovered dietary factors that can kill them, at least in some forms of cancer.

Foods such as: purple potatoes, green tea, walnuts and extra virgin olive oil.

Other foods that attack cancer stem cells are: The ketogenic diet

To crown it all, stem cells still work, but as they age, they slow down and may need help. Eating foods that mobilize your stem cells can increase your body's intrinsic ability to protect and maintain your organs. Regenerative nutrition, which stimulates stem cells from within, is a whole new way of thinking about the foods and beverages we eat every day.

Keep in mind that Mediterranean and Asian diets often contain ingredients that have been proven to help stem cells. And keep in mind that other diets, such as diets high in fat, salt or sugar, can stun them, this is not something you want to do often. If you're fighting a chronic disease, activating your stem cells can be important to help you overcome the damage to your tissues. If you have had a heart attack or stroke, your stem cells can help you save your heart and rebuild your brain. In these situations, the growth of stem cells is a way to fight for your health, to regain strength and maintain the functioning of your body at any time of life.

If you want to improve your fitness, eating regenerative foods will help you improve blood flow and have more energy and better resistance. If you are an athlete or you are practicing any kind of physical performance, you will need to recruit these stem cells to develop your muscle. If you are middle aged and want your body to stay young, if you have had surgery and want to be healed quickly, or if you are recovering from an illness and want to recover quickly, consume foods that increase the volume of your stem cells can be a way to reach your goals.

Finally, not all stem cells are your friends, cancer stem cells are extremely dangerous. If you have cancer or have ever had cancer, your main goal should be to kill cancer stem cells. There is still no drug that can do this, but more and more foods, as well as their bioactive substances, are being investigated for their suppressor effects on cancer stem cells. Fortunately, foods that attack cancer stem cells do not harm beneficial stem cells.

Chapter 8

Feed your internal ecosystem

Key takeaway

1. The best way to consume bacteria is to add more dietary fiber to your diet and less protein and animal fat.

2. We all need to make these better decisions when we sit down to feed ourselves, because we never eat for one or two, but for $ 39 trillion. This is the amount of bacteria that make up the microbiome in our body.

3. When it comes to healthy eating, it's not just about you. Also take care of your microbiome.

We all need to make these better decisions when we sit down to feed ourselves, because we never eat for one or two, but for $ 39 trillion. This is the number of bacteria that make up the microbiome in our body.

Well nourishing our gut bacteria begins a biochemical domino effect that not only influences our digestion but also our overall health. A well-maintained community of gut bacteria will affect your ability to withstand diseases such as cancer and diabetes, your ability to heal wounds and ask your brain to release chemicals that make it more sociable. A gut bacterium called Akkermansia muciniphila constitutes between 1 and 3% of all bacteria in the intestinal microbiome. But this small population has a big impact. Akkermansia can help control the immune system, improve blood sugar metabolism, reduce intestinal inflammation and fight against obesity. The cranberry and pomegranate juice data show how powerful our diet can influence our microbiome, which can also influence our immune response to cancer treatment, with vital implications for life or death.

Changes in the microbiome, known as dysbiosis, are found in severe health conditions, ranging from obesity to metabolic syndrome, to type 2 diabetes, and so on. These conditions have abnormalities and lesions of gut bacteria associated with poor dietary habits, environmental factors and the use of antibiotics. Cancer, particularly in the organs of the gastrointestinal tract (stomach, esophagus, pancreas, gallbladder, colon and rectum) is associated with microbiological disorders. People with Parkinson's disease and Alzheimer's also observe disorders of the intestinal microbiome. New evidence shows that harmful bacteria that develop in the gut can produce neurotoxins that cause inflammation of the brain.

Foods that contain healthy bacteria

Many foods contain healthy bacteria used to ferment foods and prevent them from spoiling. Even today, living cultures of bacteria are essential for the production of many common foods. Eating fermented foods can increase the diversity of your gut microbiome, which improves your health defenses. Here are some of the foods based on bacteria.

Food like:

Sauerkraut

Sauerkraut is a bitter, sour and tasty accompaniment to many traditional foods, and is sometimes used as a pleasure-like condiment. It is incredibly rich in microbes, made by fermenting cabbage in very thin slices with bacteria producing lactic acid (Lactobacilli).

kimchi

Everyone who enjoyed Korean food have probably eaten kimchi, a tasty and spicy staple of salted fermented vegetables like radishes, Napa cabbage, peppers, onions, garlic, ginger and fermented seafood called jeotgal .

Pao Cai (Chinese fermented cabbage)

Pao cai (pronounced "pow tsai") is a traditional dish of fermented vegetables in China, often found in Chinese restaurants as a cold snack. Like kimchi, pao cai is made from healthy vegetables: carrots, cabbage, radish, green mustard stalks, and ginger.

Cheese

Regarding the microbiome, cheese is good for the gut. The cheese is made with milk, an enzyme called rennet and a starter culture. The starter is made up of different types of bacteria, depending on the type of cheese made.

Yogurt

Yogurt is made with milk that is heated, cooled and mixed with bacteria for fermentation.

Sourdough bread

Bread is a staple all over the world, and archaeologists have discovered that primitive humans did it 14,000 years ago, before farming began, making it an authentic "paleo meal" ".

Taking care of your microbiome

The guiding principles for taking care of your gut microbiome follow three basic rules: Eat a lot of dietary fiber from whole foods. Eat less animal protein Eat more fresh, whole foods and less processed foods.

The foods that have a beneficial effect on your microbiome are:

Pumpernickel Bread, Kiwifruit, Brassica (like broccoli, cauliflower, bok choy, cabbage, kale, rutabaga, turnips, and arugula), *Bamboo Shoots, Dark Chocolate, Walnuts, Beans, Mushrooms,* Beverages (like *Fruit Juices: Pomegranate, Cranberry, and Concord Grape), Red Wine and Teas.*

So far I'm mainly focused on foods that can add to your diet that actively make you healthier, rather than foods that need to be eliminated, but when it comes to the microbiome, I want to address a substance that can be better avoided: artificial sweeteners. The artificial sweeteners currently approved for human consumption are aspartame, saccharin, sucralose, acesulfame and neotame.

Chapter 9
Direct your Genetic Fate

Key takeaway

1. Eating foods containing antioxidants is just one aspect of protecting your genetic code.
2. A conscious diet containing foods with protective properties of DNA can increase the defenses of your health.

Pollution, industrial toxins, ultraviolet light and emotional stress are damaging our genetic code. When DNA is damaged, genes can malfunction. The consequences, such as aging, wrinkled skin, may be visible. Or, the effects can be insidious and invisible, causing cancer or damaging the brain, heart, lungs and other organs. But food and drinks can help protect your own DNA from environmental attack and natural mutations.

When we read about food and health, we often talk about antioxidants. Many foods contain bioactive chemicals with antioxidant properties. Often these foods and their antioxidants are praised for their ability to neutralize free radicals, reduce cellular stress and protect DNA.

Scientific and clinical evidence of the foods that protect our DNA and how they really work. Vitamin C, one of the most commonly consumed dietary supplements, is found naturally in many foods of plant origin. The study found that eating orange juice improves the blood's ability to protect DNA. The good news is that antioxidants are not the only mechanism to prevent damage to our genes. Food can trigger naturally occurring health defenses in our DNA. Some foods can speed up the repair of broken DNA once the damage is done. What we eat can also activate or deactivate certain genes through so-called epigenetic modifications. In addition to diet, exercise, sleep, and environmental exposures can also have good (and bad) epigenetic effects. But foods that have a positive epigenetic influence can trigger beneficial genes or disable those that are harmful to prevent and fight disease.

DNA is damaged in many serious diseases, including all types of cancer. Skin cancer is perhaps the most common, caused by solar radiation (UV) that damages the DNA in every part of the exposed skin (think: sunburn on the beach). This is a process called "cancerization in the field". Other cancers are linked to occupational, environmental and food exposures in which DNA is repeatedly damaged in specific organs. These include cancers of the esophagus, bladder, lung, stomach and colon, where attacks of air and diet can alter your DNA.

Infections by bacteria and viruses that cause diseases can cause genetic mutations that can occur tumors and cervical cancer, liver cancer (hepatocellular) and cancer of the mouth and upper respiratory tract. Some people have inherited mutations in which the body has weakened the mechanisms of DNA repair. For these people, cancer is a very likely fate.

Autoimmune diseases cause DNA damage, not only in organs affected by a hyperactive immune system, but also in white blood cells circulating in the blood.

Epigenetic changes can be harmful, but also useful, and occur during a person's life. Changes in DNA expression can be passed from generation to generation. Researchers finds out that these changes play a role in a remarkable variety of diseases such as schizophrenia, Alzheimer's disease, autism spectrum disorder, Parkinson's disease, major depression, atherosclerosis and autoimmune diseases.

Foods that influence DNA repair

Foods that influence DNA include vitamins A, B, C, D, and E, found in carrots, spinach, red peppers, lentils, navy beans, and mushrooms, as well as eggs, sardines, cod liver oil and mackerel. Minerals like magnesium, found in oatmeal, almonds, bananas and tofu and zinc found in oysters, crab and lobster, are needed to maintain DNA repair mechanisms.

It becomes clear that the benefits of whole foods are greater than those any individual element, be it a vitamin, a mineral or even a bioactive. Foods such as:

Berry juice: berry juice is ubiquitous, from groceries to juice bars and smoothie stands. Red berries and black berries contain many bioactive substances, including anthocyanins and other polyphenols with antioxidant effects.

Kiwi: the kiwi has a beneficial impact on the microbiome. The kiwifruit also contains high levels of vitamin C, chlorogenic acid and quinic acid which have antioxidant effects.

Carrots: carrots are rich in bioactive called carotenoids reds and yellow pigments found in the world of herbal food. Carotenoids are potent with respect to antioxidant activity.

Broccoli: Eating broccoli is good for your health and one of its benefits is DNA protection

Foods rich in lycopene: watermelon, tomato, guava, pink grapefruit:

The next time you go to the beach, consider having a glass of tomato juice, watermelon, pink grapefruit or guava before you leave. This will protect you from sun damage. The red-orange color of these fruits comes from lycopene, which protects the DNA from damage caused by ionizing radiation from the sun.

Seafood: In addition to its anti-angiogenic effects, the polyunsaturated fatty acids (PUFA omega-3) crustaceans can protect your DNA. The next time you are in the fish market or a restaurant, consider these main sources of marine omega-3 PUFAs for their benefits on DNA repair: hake (a white-fleshed fish of the cod family), sea cucumber (a delicacy in Asia, linked to the starfish), manila clams and cockles, tuna (beware of high mercury level), yellow tail and bottarga (dried mullet eggs considered a delicacy in the Mediterranean).

Oysters from the Pacific: oysters protect your DNA. Among more than one hundred varieties of salted bivalves, the Pacific oyster is a relatively small and sweet oyster, widely cultivated and consumed around the world. They do not produce pearls, but they offer antioxidant benefits.

Foods with epigenetic effects

Beyond the protection or repair of DNA, foods can affect the function of DNA through a process called epigenetic change. Remember, epigenetic influences are those that come from external exposures, such as food or the environment. These influences can trigger DNA that would otherwise be silent and that would not work, or block DNA that would otherwise be active. Foods with epigenetic effects include: cruciferous vegetables, soybeans, tea, coffee, turmeric, herbs.

Foods that protect the telomeres

Telomeres play an important role in protecting your DNA by protecting the ends of your chromosomes from damage. Telomeres naturally shorten with age, as a fuse burning down. Any action that helps them stay longer will help protect your DNA and fight against aging. Foods that protect telomeres include: tea, coffee, nuts and seeds, the Mediterranean diet and Asian diets rich in vegetables.

Foods that damage our defense mechanisms of DNA health

Some foods are not as good for your DNA and even help to damage them. It is important that we inform you of diet and eating habits that may damage our DNA. Foods such as: PROCESSED MEAT, FATTY FOOD, and SUGAR BEVERAGES.

Live the good life is full of dangers for your DNA. You cannot avoid all the damage, because aging inevitably takes its victims. But you can consciously use your food options as countermeasures to protect, repair and correct your DNA to defend your health. It's easy to make daily decisions about what foods to take.

Foods containing bioactive substances that are antioxidants can neutralize harmful oxidizing chemicals in the blood. But remember, this only protects the DNA from damage. Some foods can actually help repair DNA by activating cellular machinery to solve problems. Foods with epigenetic effects can influence your DNA by releasing genes that protect your health, such as tumor suppressor genes that prevent the growth of cancer cells. Using your DNA in this way could literally save your life.

Finally, foods that protect and extend telomeres can protect your DNA and help combat the effects of aging. While telomeres are reduced throughout our lives and expose our DNA to damage, dietary habits can reduce this reduction and, in some cases, even extend telomeres. Your DNA is not just a model of your genetic code, it's a super information highway that needs to be protected, repaired and, in some cases, redirected to combat the attacks of our environment and the ravages of aging, to defend our health.

Chapter 10
Activate your immune command center

Key takeaway

1. A strong immune defense can protect against a large number of diseases outside the body, such as infections, but it can also defend against diseases developed internally, such as cancer or autoimmune diseases.

2. A diet that stimulates the immune system during cancer treatment can contribute to the success of your medical treatments.

3. Autoimmune diseases are serious conditions in which your immune system is too aggressive and can cause serious or even fatal damage to your organs.

With regard to their immunity, certain food traditions are now being examined from the new angle of the defense of health. The science of modern immunology reveals which foods affect immunity and tells us how they work. New discoveries reveal that specific foods can help improve your immune system, keep it in top shape, and fight the disease. There is a simple way to understand the impact of the diet on the immune system. What we eat and drink can increase or decrease the two arms of immunity, the innate and acquired immune system, to defend our health.

Immunity-related diseases are the first, the conditions in which the immune system is weakened and cannot prevent invaders from taking root. Second, there are the conditions in which the immune system is excessively accelerated and its exuberance causes inflammation and the involuntary destruction of our own healthy tissues.

A damaged immune system can open the door to life-threatening infections, but infection is just a danger. Cancer can also take root because an inefficient immune system cannot detect cancer cells. This weakness can be corrected by cancer treatments called immunotherapies, new drugs that help the immune system locate and destroy cancer cells.

These FDA-approved therapies can help your body's immune system detect and destroy cancer. The irony is that traditional cancer treatments based on high doses of chemotherapy and radiation actually weaken the immune system. They destroy fast-growing cells, which is an effective way to fight cancer. But immune cells and other healthy cells are also decimated during treatment, which prevents the body from defending against cancer. Infection with some viruses can also destroy the body's ability to develop an adequate immune response.

Some diseases really paralyze the immune system. Although types 1 and 2 of diabetes are different types of diseases, both factors make an individual more vulnerable to infections. The overactivity of immunity is the consequence of autoimmune diseases in which the immune system is active in the wrong place at the wrong time, causing chronic inflammation and organ damage.

Foods that stimulate the immune system

Foods that stimulate immune function include: aged garlic, mushrooms, broccoli sprouts, extra virgin olive oil and ellagic acid (chestnuts, blackberries, black raspberries, nuts and pomegranates).

Fruit juice with immune power

Fruit juices that can boost immune power include: Concord grape juice, cranberry juice, cranberries, peppers, Pacific oysters and licorice.

Foods that calm inflammation and autoimmunity

Autoimmune diseases are seemingly insoluble diseases that doctors treat with high doses of steroids to suppress immunity. But the problem with steroids is that they have side effects that lead to unexpected consequences, such as weakening of the bones, thinning of the skin, cataract formation, damage to wound healing and even psychosis. Steroids, while often effective, are at best an imperfect solution. Eating foods that domesticate the immune system is an important step for people with autoimmune disease. A dietary approach can help protect organs from destruction by friendly fire from their own immune system, as well as drugs used to treat autoimmune diseases. Some foods can alleviate the suffering of autoimmune diseases by reducing inflammation.

Foods containing vitamin C can help reduce the body's autoimmune response, including green tea, raw vegan diet, and a diet rich in vegetables (high) and low protein.

PART 3: PLAN, CHOOSE, AND ACT
Putting Food to work

Right now, it's time to improve the way you approach food and choose what you eat. Every day, several times a day, you make important decisions that can tip the scales in your favor to live longer and better without a dreaded chronic illness.

Thanks to the 5 × 5 × 5 frame, it makes it easy to integrate healthy foods into your daily life. This approach is not a one size-fits-all diet, nor a plan to lose weight. It's a simple way to help you make healthy decisions in a conscious and systematic way, no matter what you do or where you live.

Chapter 11

The 5x5x5 FRAMEWORK: Eating to Beat Disease

Are you ready to take action to make your body healthier and better able to fight disease?

This 5 x 5 x 5 frame is not a plan to lose weight, a physical diet or a plan of mental clarity. It's not a meal-by-meal, or a day-by-day plan that tells you how to live your life strictly. It's much better. This plan has to do with freedom, because I will not tell you until the last thing you have to eat (or not eat) every day. Instead, I am going to offer you a fun new way to integrate health and defense-type foods into your lifestyle that will give you a better look, a feeling of well-being and a longer life.

The 5 × 5 × 5 framework is a strategy that I have developed to support the five health advocacy systems by working at least a minimum of five health-supporting foods you already like to eat into meals and snacks and incorporate them into 5 times per day, into the opportunities where you eat or snack: breakfast, lunch, dinner, and a few moments when you eat snacks or eat dessert.

However, the 5 × 5 × 5 is a framework, not a prescription, it fits any diets you currently follow, be it Paleo, Whole30, Ornish, low-carb, gluten-free, allergen-free, plants-based or ketogenic, and it's easy to adopt if you do not follow a plan at all. The 5 × 5 × 5 framework does not exclude anyone because it is a broader concept in which you can easily integrate other protocols. Everyone can do it.

The 5 × 5 × 5 framework is flexible and requires little implementation effort, which facilitates compliance. And it's not restrictive. It's about adding beneficial foods to your diet, without excluding foods. The 5 × 5 × 5 frame works because it is not perfection; it's a question of choice. The daily choices count, and above all, they add up!

How to use the 5 × 5 × 5 framework

1. First, use the list of foods below and identify the ones you prefer from more than 200 products that benefit at least one of the five health advocacy

systems. This helps you create your personalized list of favorite foods.

2. Next, choose five foods to eat each day. Make sure that each of them supports at least one of the defense systems and that it covers the five systems of these five food options.

3. Finally, eat five foods a day for one or all of the five meals, snacks or other "occasions" you eat. Most people have 5 encounter a day with food (breakfast, lunch, snack, dinner, dessert) and it may be easier to incorporate the foods chosen on all five occasions. But you can eat them together in groups. You can eat as often as you like, depending on your personal preferences. Just make sure you eat the five foods each day.

Some guiding principles have been used to develop this framework.

Life is not always perfect

Positive food choices reinforce your health defenses, but you will sometimes be in a situation where the right choices are neither easy nor possible. That's why regularly making good decisions can help balance the effects of unhealthy choices that we all make occasionally.

But if you're in the yellow or red zone and you cannot make healthy choices, it's worth coming back as fast as you can to control your choices in your 5 × 5 × 5 framework.

Eat what you like

The 5 × 5 × 5 framework gives you the freedom to choose what you eat and when you eat it. The starting point is to select your favorite foods from a list of foods known to improve your defense systems. These foods are part of your personalized health framework - you can choose them. Everyone prefers to eat the foods they like.

The 5 × 5 × 5 frame is designed to avoid the problem of boredom by constantly eating the same things. It's easier to follow healthy habits when eating what you already love.

Customize

There is no single approach to health that is correct for everyone. Doctors know that in the future, our work with patients will be more and more personalized.

SUMMARY: EAT TO BEAT DISEASE By William W Li

But it is not necessary to wait until the future begins to benefit from a personalized approach to health. You can create your own solutions using the 5 × 5 × 5 framework by adopting a personalized diet each day, taking into account your tastes and preferences, food allergies and sensitivities, risks and concerns for health, the circumstances of life, the budget and any eventuality and whatever else that matters to you.

Make it sustainable

The 5x5x5 framework is durable because it personal, it is based on your tastes and adaptability to circumstances of life- so you can stick to it.

Be adaptable

The frame 5x5x5 framework is designed to be flexible and adaptable to any situation according to the evolution of life. The options you have in a restaurant vary a lot from the ones you have in your own kitchen.

Implement the 5 × 5 × 5 framework

The 5 × 5 × 5 framework brings together all the information you have learned in this book in a simple action plan that will improve your health, satisfy your taste buds and protect you against disease.

Each of the three 5s represents an action you can take for your health:

5 health defense systems
5 health-defending foods to select each day
5 opportunities to eat them each day

We will define them.

The First 5 in 5 × 5 × 5: The Health Defense Systems

There are five health defense systems in your body: angiogenesis, regeneration, microbiome, DNA protection and immunity. These systems maintain your health in a state of perfect balance. If you do something for each system each day, it will strengthen your general resistance to the disease and develop a life habit to cover your basics.

The Second 5 in 5 × 5 × 5: Health-Defending Foods

The second 5 is your choice of at least five favorite foods to include in your diet each day.

You do not need permission to eat what you like. Surprisingly, when you choose five different foods to attack each of the five health defense systems every day, you get a total of 35 healthy foods a week, or 1,820 healthy food options in one year!

If you follow the 5 × 5 × 5 framework, 95% of your food choices will stay healthy. Once again, the good choices outweigh the bad ones.

To be clear, these are not the only five foods you will eat each day, but rather the five foods you choose to deliberately add with any other food you eat during a day. In addition, they are probably not the same five foods every day.

If you wish, you can repeat the exercise from day to day, but the goal is to eat at least five a day. Of course, this does not limit your health choices. You can have as many healthy ingredients as you want. The more you stack one healthy food on another, the more it feeds your strength and strengthens your health care.

The Third 5 in 5 × 5 × 5: Opportunities to Eat the Health Defense Foods

The latter 5 refers to when we eat: meals and snacks. The fact is that most of us eat five times a day: breakfast, lunch and dinner, and possibly a snack and dessert. This means that you receive five injections a day to eat the five healthy foods you have chosen. You can choose to eat the five daily choices at a meal or distribute them at certain meals. This allows you the flexibility to adapt healthy eating into changing circumstances, even when you travel and you may need to skip a meal.

Once you have started, you will find that it is very easy to do because it is flexible, customizable, realistic and creates habits. More importantly, it is rooted in your preferences.

Let us get started.
STEP 1: Create your personalized list of favorite foods

For the 5 × 5 × 5 framework, start by creating your own favorite food list (PFL) based on the foods you really like. You create your list from the main list of all the following foods.

Preferred Foods List
Fruits: Acerola, Apples (Red Delicious), Apples (Reinnette), Bitter melon, Apples (Granny Smith), Apricot, Black plums, Black raspberries (dried), Blackberries (dried), Blueberries (dried), Camu camu, Cherries (dried), Cranberries (dried), Grapefruit,

Guava, Lychee, Nectarines, Papaya, Persimmon, Plums, Raspberries, Watermelon, Black chokeberry, Black raspberries, Blackberries, Blueberries, Cherries, Cranberries, Goji berries, Grapes, Kiwifruit, Mangoes, Oranges, Peaches, Pink grapefruit, Pomegranates, Strawberries, Sultana raisins.

Vegetables such as: Arugula, Bamboo shoots, Bok choy, Broccoli rabe, Cabbage, Carrots, Celery, Chicory Chile peppers, Collard greens, Escarole, Frisee, Kale, Mustard greens, Pao cai, Purple potatoes, Red-leaf lettuce, Romanesco, San Marzano tomatoes, Spinach, Swiss chard, Tardivo di Treviso, Turnips, Watercress, Aged garlic, Asparagus, Belgian endive, Broccoli, Broccoli sprouts, Capers, Cauliflower, Cherry tomatoes, Chinese celery, Eggplant, Fiddleheads, Green beans, Kimchi, Onions, Puntarelle, Radicchio, Red black-skin tomatoes, Rutabaga, Sauerkraut, Squash blossoms, Tangerine tomatoes, Tomatoes *and* Wasabi.

Legumes/Fungi such as: Chanterelle mushrooms, Enoki mushrooms, Lion's mane mushrooms, Morel mushrooms, Oyster mushrooms, Porcini mushrooms, Soy, White button mushrooms, Black beans, Chickpeas, Lentils, Maitake mushrooms, Navy beans, Peas, Shiitake mushrooms *and* Truffles

Nuts, Seeds, Whole Grains, Bread: Almonds, Brazil nuts, Cashews, Chia seeds, Hazelnuts, Peanut butter, Pecans, Pistachios, Pumpkin seeds, Sesame seeds, Squash seeds, Tahini, Whole grains, Almond butter, Barley, Cashew butter, Chestnuts, Flax seeds, Macadamia nuts, Peanuts, Pine nuts, Pumpernickel bread, Rice bran, Sourdough bread, Sunflower seeds *and* Walnuts.

Seafood: Arctic char, Black bass, Bluefish, Caviar (sturgeon), Eastern oysters, Gray mullet, Halibut, Mackerel, Mediterranean sea bass, Pacific oysters, Rainbow trout, Red mullet, Salmon, Sea bream, Spiny lobster, Swordfish, Yellowtail (fish), Anchovies, Bigeye tuna, Bluefin tuna, Bottarga, Cockles (clam), Fish roe (salmon), Hake, John Dory (fish), Manila clam, Oyster sauce, Pompano, Razor clams, Redfish, Sardine, Sea cucumber, Squid ink *and* Tuna.

Meat: Chicken (dark meat)

Dairy: Cheddar cheese, Emmenthal cheese, Jarlsberg cheese, Parmigiano-Reggiano, Yogurt, Camembert cheese, Edam cheese, Gouda cheese, Muenster cheese *and* Stilton cheese

Spices/Herbs: Cinnamon, Licorice root, Oregano, Rosemary, Sage, Turmeric, Basil, Ginseng, Marjoram, Peppermint, Saffron **and** Thyme.

Oil: Olive oil (EVOO)

Sweets: Dark chocolate

Beverages: Beer, Chamomile tea, Black tea, Coffee, Cranberry juice, Jasmine tea, Oolong tea, Pomegranate juice, Sencha green tea, Cloudy, apple cider, Concord grape juice, Green tea, Mixed berry juice, Orange juice, Red wine (Cabernet, Cabernet Franc, Petit Verdot).

STEP 2: snap it

Now that you've identified your favorite foods, it's time to highlight how your preferences help every health advocacy. Create daily worksheet 5x5x5. The worksheet should include several pages listing the foods under the heading of their defense systems: angiogenesis, regeneration, microbiome, DNA protection and immunity. Take the list from Step 1 and transfer the markers you marked from Step 1 into the worksheet under the defense system you activate. Do not worry if some of the foods you check appear multiple times on the spreadsheet. This is because there are foods that influence several defense systems. Mark the food you prefer each time it appears on the worksheet.

Once you have transferred your favorite foods to the worksheet, take out your cell phone and take a picture of each page of the worksheet. Now it's a recording of your personal favorite 5 × 5 × 5 (PFL) list that you can take with you and refer to where ever you go.

STEP 3: Choose five each day

You are now ready to set the entire 5 × 5 × 5 framework to motion. Each day of the week, you examine your PFL and select five different foods, one in each category of defense. It's good if some foods influence more than one defense system. These five foods are what you will be assigned to eat that day. In this way, you will support each of the five defense systems on a daily basis.

STEP 4: Eat the Five

Now you are ready to put it in action. Go get the five foods you have chosen and eat them at the times you choose. Flexibility is important because your schedule and the ease of eating certain foods can change from day to day and from situation to situation. Everything depends on you. The key is to activate the five health defense systems each day.

STEP 5: navigate your life

One of the questions I get often is: Is this framework compatible with paleo, pescatarian, ketogenic, vegetarian, vegan, gluten-free or dairy-free restrictions, or with any other restrictions? The answer is yes. If you follow a specific food philosophy, you can still use this frame because the food choices on the list of favorite foods are very broad. You only need to become familiar with foods that may not have been in your diet and remove them from your list of preferences.

Tips for incorporating the 5 × 5 × 5 structure

To help you incorporate the 5 × 5 × 5 frame into your life, here are some expert tips.

1. Try to leave the Club Clean plate

2. You have to skip meals every week

3. Try to eat carefully

4. Try to eat with the people you love

5. Always try a new recipe

Chapter 12

Rethinking the Kitchen

Key takeaway

You need the right tools to prepare and cook your food, as well as the right ingredients in your pantry.

Now that you know how to create your own 5 × 5 × 5 framework, you will need tools to launch it, starting in your kitchen. You can be one of those people who lead such a busy life busy life that you dine out most of the time, and that's not the best path to health. Having the tools to prepare a healthy meal or snack at home makes personal health easier.

To eat to fight the disease, you must choose the right foods, store them properly and prepare them in the way that best suits your health. These are important not only for flavor and food safety. The proper cooking process can help maintain or even enhance the health benefits of its ingredients.

A healthy diet starts with fresh, high quality ingredients. But once you have them, you must know how to cook them. Many cooking techniques can be used to prepare healthy foods, but some are easier to cook for the home than others.

Chapter 13
Exceptional Food

Key takeaway

1. The food you are about to read is one of the exceptional foods that I think is worth testing. Not only do they support your health defenses, but they can also stimulate your taste buds.

I will summarize some of the foods I consider exceptional, based on their culinary and their health virtues. Consider this as a full version of the Eat to Beat Disease playlist. I encourage you to look for them and give them a try. These foods can not only fit easily into your 5 × 5 × 5 framework, but they will open your mind and palate to exciting new flavors.

The first is "Global Finds", which includes lesser known foods that have not been found yet, let alone proven.

Second, there are the "Jaw-Droppers," foods whose benefits are surprising.

Third, I will introduce you to the "Grand Slammers". These are the foods that affect not only one or two, but the five health defense systems.

Finally, the "Market Highlights". This section takes you on a virtual tour of the market and tells you how to buy as an expert to get the best of the best.

Global Finds includes: Squash blossoms, Fresh wasabi, Persimmons, Fiddleheads, Bitter melon, Truffles, Bottarga, Razor clams and Squid ink.

Jaw-Droppers includes:
Cheese, Beer, Chocolate, Prosciutto and jamón, Spicy food, Tree nuts and Purple potato.

Grand Slammers includes:

Keep in mind that there are many other foods and ingredients that promote the defense of health that you can eat with these Grand Slammers. I recommend you do not focus too much on them and try to combine different foods to mix things and keep your diet interesting and diverse.

Fruits: Blueberries, Kiwifruit, Mangoes, Plums, Apricots, Cherries,

Lychee, Nectarines **and** Peaches

Vegetables: Carrots, Fiddleheads, Kale, Bamboo shoots **and** Eggplant.

Beverages: Chamomile tea, Green tea, Black tea **and** Coffee.

Nuts/Seeds: Pumpkin seeds, Walnuts, Flax seed, Sesame seeds **and** Sunflower seeds.

Seafood: Squid ink

Oils: Olive oil (EVOO)

Sweets: Dark chocolate

Market Highlights

Shopping at the grocery store or at the market may seem repetitive and it's easy to get caught up in the routine.

If this actually describes your experience, you may find that buying food is so boring. You know there must be other better options, but you may not know which ones to choose. The PFL you have created will give you a variety of colorful and delicious options.

Chapter 14
Simple Meal Guide

It is useful to have a guide or a template to follow to become familiar and comfortable when creating your own approach to diet with the 5x5x5 framework.

Eating to defeat the disease will only be effective if you have a plan that you can follow. Your plan must take into account the realities of everyday life. Rigid diets are therefore difficult to maintain. For this reason, I deliberately designed the $5 \times 5 \times 5$ framework to allow the fact that, despite our best intentions, our days and weeks do not always go as planned.

Chapter 15

Food Doses

Key takeaway

1. If we view foods as drugs, then food must have doses.

2. Balance is your health goal.

3. Eating foods that improve health defenses can be even more important as we get older.

A dose of food is the amount of food or drink consumed associated with or leads to a specific health outcome. Like the (bio) chemical components of drugs, the bioactives of the foods you consume have specific pharmacological effects on your cells. As we have seen throughout this book, foods are studied using some of the same methods as those used in drug development. I want to put it at the forefront of the "Food as a medicine" movement and show it how the concept of food dosage shapes the future of how we will use food to fight disease. The first step is to discover the correct doses for foods that will help us improve our health. When it comes to drugs, doctors know that it's important to know which drug is the right drug and the right dose to get the best results.

I explain how specific foods can be useful because, like medicine, the bioactives they contain can influence our cells and the biological systems of our body in the same way as drugs. I share what I know about the importance of food selection and how to prepare food to get the most out of their health benefits.

In the science of food dosing, we start with the amounts of a food identified by clinical studies or epidemiological surveys of eating habits reported by large populations and analyze their beneficial effect on health. We analyze the data to see if the benefits associated with food match what we know about the bioactive components of food in health advocacy systems, and act to help maintain health and ward off disease. Then we translate the quantity of food or drink declared as consumed and its frequency in doses.

We study foods as a drug by analyzing actual bioactive substances in food and we observe their effects in laboratory studies that use molecular, genetic and biochemical tests commonly used for biopharmaceutical research. The activities of these substances are then converted into quantities in foods to determine if the required food dose would be realistic to consume.

So far, most references to the amount of a "healthy" food have focused on serving size (usually related to a weight loss goal). But today, we can apply new tools in molecular, cellular and genomic biology to explore how foods can contribute to health in a way that was not possible a few years ago.

Five important warnings to keep in mind when choosing a dose of food:

First, most studies are conducted through epidemiological research, which makes it possible to use real populations of people like you and me, to look for associations between reported or researched eating habits and specific health outcomes.

Second, most clinical studies on specific foods and health effects (high blood pressure, blood glucose control, heart disease) are small studies. They therefore involve relatively few people, perhaps only a few dozen or even fewer.

Third, we learn from the vanguard of personalized medicine that each person is different. We all have our own microbiomes, both genetic and epigenetic. Everyone metabolizes food differently. When we eat combinations of foods, their bioactive substances combine in our body to produce effects different from those that we could expect with a single food. This means that even when studying a large number of individuals, one cannot predict whether an individual will respond to a particular food in the same way.

Fourth, remember that if you are currently struggling with an illness, you should consult your doctor before changing the way you eat.

Fifth, the most important reason why you should take a broader and more flexible approach to diet and health are at the center of concern because there is no quick fix to avoid all diseases. Food can be seen in many ways for the same purpose as drugs, but the complex nature of these means that food can achieve health in ways drugs cannot.

The fact is that if the defenses against the health of your body are perfectly prepared and functioning, you will have a good chance of avoiding the next disease: cardiovascular diseases, Cancer, Diabetes, Obesity Autoimmune disease, Diseases of aging. It is these chronic diseases that kill millions of people every year, cause untold suffering and overburden our health systems. Many of these diseases are directly related to lifestyle. To succeed, we must involve several defense systems to prevent or modify the disease properly. No food does everything. You must gather all the defense systems of your body.